TEACHING YOUR KIDS TO BE GOOD HUMANS

Book 1: THE POWER OF SELF-CONTROL

TEACHING KIDS TO MANAGE THEIR EMOTIONS

CREATED BY
KIMM REID, BAPSYCH

The Power of Self Control ©Kimm Reid 2023

Reserved: No part of this book may be reproduced without the written permission of the Publisher.

ISBN: 978-1-988001-78-4

Published and Printed in the United States of America

Book One in the Teaching Your Kids to be Good Humans Series

Book Two: The Case for Compassion
Book Three: The Art of Empathy
Book Four: The Secret of Motivation
Book Five: The Strength of Tenacity
Book Six: The Value of Respect
Book Seven: The Virtue of Honesty
Book Eight: The Magic of Kindness

Created by
Kimm Reid, BAPych

Outline:

Introduction:

- Why teaching self-control is important for kids
- Common challenges parents face in teaching self-control
- Overview of the book's contents

Chapter 1: Understanding Self-Control
- What is self-control?
- How self-control develops in children
- The benefits of self-control for children

Chapter 2: Teaching Self-Control to Young Children
- Strategies for teaching self-control to young children
- Common mistakes to avoid when teaching self-control
- How to set realistic expectations for your child's self-control development

Chapter 3: Building Emotional Awareness
- How emotional awareness relates to self-control
- Strategies for helping children identify and label emotions
- The role of empathy in teaching emotional awareness

Chapter 4: Developing Self-Regulation Skills
- What self-regulation is and why it matters
- Strategies for helping children regulate their emotions and behavior
- How to address challenging behaviors and tantrums

Chapter 5: Discipline and Positive Reinforcement
- The importance of discipline and positive reinforcement in teaching self-control
- Strategies for encouraging positive behavior and reinforcing self-control
- How to address misbehaviour and promote positive behavior

Chapter 6: Supporting Self-Control in Daily Life
- How to support your child's self-control development in everyday situations
- Strategies for promoting self-control during mealtimes, playtime, and bedtime
- The role of routines and environment in supporting self-control

Chapter 7: Nurturing Self-Esteem and Resilience
- How self-esteem and resilience relate to self-control
- Strategies for promoting self-esteem and resilience in young children
- How to foster a growth mindset in children

Conclusion:
- Recap of the book's key points
- Final thoughts on teaching self-control to young children
- Additional resources for parents, including worksheets

Introduction:

As parents, we all want our children to grow up happy, healthy, and well-adjusted. One of the most important skills we can teach our children is self-control—the ability to manage their emotions, behaviors, and impulses healthily and constructively. This skill will serve them well throughout their lives, helping them navigate challenges, build positive relationships, and achieve their goals.

This book will explore the importance of teaching kids to manage their emotions and provide practical strategies for parents to help their children develop this critical life skill. We'll examine parents' challenges in teaching self-control, the benefits for children, and the strategies parents can use to support their child's self-control development.

Challenges of Teaching Self-Control:

Teaching self-control to young children can be a challenging task for parents. It requires patience, consistency, and a deep understanding of child development. One of the main challenges parents face is setting realistic expectations for their child's development. Children develop at different rates, and parents need to recognize that self-control is a skill that takes time and practice to develop. Furthermore, if a parent has more than one child, it is crucial to understand each child will develop these skills at their own pace. It is a wise parent who realizes each child develops differently and not to push one to be like another.

Another challenge is finding effective strategies for teaching self-control. There is no one-size-fits-all approach; what works for one child may not work for another. Parents must be flexible and try different techniques to find what works best for each of their children individually.

Finally, parents may struggle with their own emotions and reactions when their child misbehaves or struggles with self-control. Parents must remain calm, patient, and understanding in these situations, as children often model their behavior after their parents.

Benefits of Self-Control for Children:

Despite the challenges, teaching self-control is a critical task for parents. Self-control is associated with many positive outcomes for children, including better academic performance, stronger social relationships, and improved mental health.

One of the critical benefits of self-control is improved academic performance. Children with better self-control can focus on their studies, resist distractions, and complete their homework on time. They are also better able to regulate their emotions and behavior in the classroom, which can lead to better relationships with teachers and peers.

Self-control is also crucial for building positive relationships with others. Children with a healthy grasp of self-control can better regulate their emotions and behaviors in social situations, leading to fewer conflicts, better communication, and more vital friendships.

Finally, self-control is vital for mental health. Children with better self-control are less likely to experience depression, anxiety, and other mental health problems. They can better cope with stress and challenges, leading to greater resilience and well-being.

Strategies for Teaching Self-Control:

Fortunately, parents can use a range of strategies to help their children develop self-control. These strategies can be tailored to each child's individual needs and developmental level. Some effective strategies include:

- <u>Building emotional awareness</u>: Helping children to identify and label their emotions at a very young age can be a powerful tool for developing self-control. By helping children to recognize their feelings and understand how they are feeling, parents can assist their little ones to regulate their emotions more effectively.

- <u>Developing self-regulation skills</u>: Self-regulation skills, such as deep breathing, mindfulness, and progressive muscle relaxation, can be powerful tools for managing emotions and promoting self-control. These skills can be taught to children early and practiced through fun activities and games.

- Positive discipline and reinforcement: Positive discipline and reinforcement can effectively encourage positive behavior and reinforce self-control. Parents can use praise, rewards, and other positive reinforcement strategies to promote positive behavior and strengthen self-control.

- Supporting self-control in daily life: Parents can support their child's self-control development in everyday situations, such as mealtime, playtime, and bedtime. By setting clear expectations and routines, parents can encourage children to develop self-control habits that will serve them well throughout their lives.

Conclusion

Teaching self-control to young children is a critical task for parents. It requires patience, consistency, and a deep understanding of child development. By setting realistic, age-appropriate expectations, building emotional awareness, and using effective strategies for promoting self-control, parents can help their children to develop these critical life skills. In the following chapters, we'll explore these strategies in more detail and provide practical guidance for parents to support their child's self-control development.

Chapter 1: Understanding Self-Control

SELF-CONTROL IS THE ABILITY TO REGULATE OUR THOUGHTS, EMOTIONS, and behaviors to align with our goals and values. It's a critical life skill that allows us to manage our impulses, delay gratification, and make thoughtful decisions. In this chapter, we'll explore what self-control is, how it develops in children, and the life-long benefits of self-control for children.

What is Self-Control?

Self-control is a complex cognitive and emotional process that involves regulating our thoughts, emotions, and behaviors to align with our goals and values. It requires us to resist immediate temptations and impulses in favor of long-term goals and values. Self-control is often described as the ability to "put the brakes" on our whims and delay gratification, for the better good of either the crowd or ourselves.

Self-control can be broken down into two key components: inhibition and activation. <u>Inhibition</u> involves resisting impulses and avoiding behaviors not aligned with our goals and values. <u>Activation</u> involves initiating behavior aligned with our goals and values, even if it requires effort or discomfort. Both components are essential for self-control and can be strengthened through practice and effort; seeing the desired results of our self-control motivates us to implement the practice to an even greater degree. This can be seen in a person, for example, who is an elite athlete such as a wrestler—they must exercise far greater self-control in the areas of food, than say a person of the same age, gender, etc. who plays sports for fun.

How Does Self-Control Develop in Children?

Self-control is not a fixed trait we are born with but rather a skill that develops over time. Children begin to develop self-control in their early years as they learn to regulate their emotions and behaviors in response to their environment.

A range of factors, including genetics, temperament, and environmental factors, influences the development of self-control. Some children may be naturally more impulsive or emotionally reactive, while others may be inherently more self-controlled. However, all children can benefit from learning and practicing self-control skills.

The development of self-control can be broken down into different stages, each with its challenges and opportunities for growth. Here are some of the critical stages of self-control development in children:

<u>Infancy (0-2 years)</u>: Infants are not capable of self-control in the traditional sense, but they are beginning to learn to regulate their emotions and behaviors through interactions with their caregivers. Infants rely on their caregivers to meet their needs and provide a safe and secure environment.

Toddlerhood (2-3 years): Toddlers are beginning to develop self-control skills but are still prone to emotional outbursts and impulsive behavior. Toddlers are learning to regulate emotions and behaviors through imitation, caregiver feedback, and trial and error. This is the main reason for temper tantrums in that the child has not yet learned self-control either in desire, demand, or emotion.

Preschool (3-5 years): Preschoolers are becoming more skilled at self-control but still struggle with impulse control and emotional regulation. Preschoolers learn to regulate emotions and behaviors through play, social interactions, and caregiver feedback. Having other caregivers at this stage is beneficial to the child's learning of self-control if that secondary caregiver (such as babysitter, preschool teacher, etc.) follows similar expectations and guidance as the main caregivers.

School Age (6-11 years): School-age children are becoming more skilled at self-control, but they still face challenges related to peer pressure, academic demands, and social expectations. School-age children are learning to regulate their emotions and behaviors through school, extracurricular activities, and feedback from parents and teachers.

Adolescence (12-18 years): Adolescents are developing more sophisticated self-control skills, but they still face challenges related to identity formation, autonomy, and peer pressure. Adolescents are learning to regulate their emotions and behaviors through social relationships, academic and career goals, and feedback from peers and mentors.

The Benefits of Self-Control for Children

Developing self-control is beneficial for children in a range of ways. Here are some of the critical benefits of self-control for children:

Academic Performance: Children with better self-control can focus on their studies, resist distractions, and complete their homework on time. They are also better able to regulate their emotions and behavior in the classroom, which can lead to better relationships with teachers and peers.

Social Relationships: Children who have better self-control are better able to regulate their emotions and behaviors in social situations, which can lead to fewer conflicts, better communication, and stronger friendships.

Mental Health: Children with better self-control are less likely to experience depression, anxiety, and other mental health problems. They can better cope with stress and challenges, leading to greater resilience and well-being.

Physical Health: Children with better self-control are less likely to engage in risky behaviors, such as drug use, alcohol use, and unsafe sex. They are also more likely to engage in healthy behaviors like regular exercise and healthy eating.

Developing self-control is a critical life skill that can benefit children in various ways. By understanding the key components of self-control and how it develops in children, parents can better support their child's self-control development and set them up for success in the future. In the following chapters, we'll explore practical strategies for teaching self-control to young children.

Chapter 2: Teaching Self-Control to Young Children

Teaching self-control to young children can be a challenging task for parents. It requires patience, consistency, and a deep understanding of child development. In this chapter, we'll explore practical strategies for teaching self-control to young children, common mistakes to avoid, and how to set realistic expectations for your child's self-control development.

Strategies for Teaching Self-Control to Young Children

1. Model Self-Control: Children learn by example, so parents must model self-control in their behavior. This means regulating your own emotions and behaviors in a way that aligns with your goals and values. For example, if you're frustrated or angry, take a deep breath and remain calm. If your child is misbehaving, avoid yelling or reacting impulsively, and instead, use positive discipline strategies to address the behavior. Allow your child to see that you are, in fact, frustrated, but that by taking certain steps such as the deep breathing, you take charge of the feelings and are in control.

2. Teach Emotional Awareness: Emotional awareness is a critical skill for self-control. Children need to understand and identify their emotions to regulate them effectively. Parents can teach emotional

awareness by labeling emotions, discussing how emotions feel in the body, and using books or games to help children understand different emotions.

3. <u>Practice Self-Regulation Skills:</u> Self-regulation skills, such as deep breathing, progressive muscle relaxation, and mindfulness, can be powerful tools for managing emotions and promoting self-control. Parents can practice these skills with their children through fun activities and games. A simple yet effective method for giving opportunity to learn these skills is through game playing. There are many emotions touched on through a board game or card game and it gives ample opportunity to teach self-regulation skills.

4. <u>Use Positive Discipline and Reinforcement:</u> Positive discipline and reinforcement can effectively encourage positive behavior and reinforce self-control. Parents can use praise, rewards, and other positive reinforcement strategies to promote positive behavior and strengthen self-control. For example, if your child can regulate their emotions during a frustrating situation, praise them for their self-control and offer a small reward, such as extra playtime or a special treat.

5. <u>Set Clear Expectations:</u> Children thrive on routine and predictability. Setting clear expectations for behavior helps children understand what is expected of them and promote self-control. Ensure your child knows what behavior is expected in different situations, such as mealtime, playtime, and bedtime. Reinforce these expectations consistently and praise your child when they are met. By clearly laying out

guidelines in different situations, you allow the child the ability to choose how to—or not to—stay within those boundaries. This gives them a place to learn *controlling self,* rather than *being controlled* from outside forces.

Common Mistakes to Avoid When Teaching Self-Control

1. <u>Being Inconsistent:</u> Consistency is vital when teaching self-control. Parents need to be consistent in their expectations, rules, and consequences. If parents are inconsistent, children will be unclear about what is expected of them, leading to frustration and misbehavior.

2. <u>Punishing Misbehavior Harshly:</u> Punishing misbehavior harshly can undermine self-control development. When children are punished severely, they may become fearful or resentful, leading to more mischief. Instead, use positive discipline strategies to address misbehavior, such as redirection, positive reinforcement, and natural consequences. Often, natural consequences are more impacting than parental instilled consequences.

3. <u>Setting Unrealistic Expectations:</u> Setting realistic expectations for your child's self-control development is essential. Self-control is a skill that takes time and practice to develop, so don't expect your child to be able to regulate their emotions ideally overnight. Set small, achievable goals for your child and reinforce their progress.

4. <u>Focusing Too Much on Punishment:</u> Punishment should be a last resort to promoting self-control. Instead, focus on positive reinforcement and teaching self-regulation skills. Punishment can undermine self-esteem and lead to resentment. In contrast, positive reinforcement can help children feel good about their progress and motivate them to continue practicing self-control.

5. <u>Overlooking the Importance of Emotional Awareness:</u> Emotional awareness is a critical self-control component. Children need to understand and identify their emotions to regulate them effectively. Make sure to spend time teaching emotional awareness and practicing self-regulation skills with your child. There is some worksheet ideas at the end to assist in your child becoming more emotionally aware.

How to Set Realistic Expectations for Your Child's Self-Control Development

Setting realistic expectations for your child's self-control development is vital for promoting success and avoiding frustration. Here are some tips for setting realistic expectations:

1. <u>Understand Your Child's Developmental Stage:</u> Children develop self-control differently depending on their age, temperament, and other factors. Please consider your child's developmental stage when

setting expectations for their self-control development. There are plenty of resources on child development across the internet.

2. **Set Small, Achievable Goals:** Self-control is a skill that takes time and practice to develop. Set small, achievable goals for your child and reinforce their progress. This can help keep your child motivated and avoid frustration.

3. **Reinforce Positive Behavior:** Reinforcing positive behavior is vital when promoting self-control. Praise your child when they demonstrate self-control and offer small rewards for progress. This can help your child feel good about their progress and motivate them to continue practicing self-control.

4. **Be Patient:** Developing self-control is a process that takes time and effort. Be patient with your child and avoid getting frustrated if they initially struggle. With consistent practice and reinforcement, your child will develop self-control over time.

Conclusion

Teaching self-control to young children is a critical task for parents. By using effective strategies for promoting self-control, avoiding common mistakes, and setting realistic expectations, parents can help their children develop this necessary life skill. By promoting self-control, parents can set their children up for academic, social, and emotional success. In the following chapters, we'll explore practical strategies for teaching self-control to young children.

Chapter 3: Building Emotional Awareness

EMOTIONAL AWARENESS IS A CRITICAL COMPONENT OF SELF-CONTROL. Children need to understand and identify their emotions to regulate them effectively. In this chapter, we'll explore how emotional awareness relates to self-control, strategies for helping children identify and label emotions, and the role of empathy in teaching emotional awareness.

How Emotional Awareness Relates to Self-Control

Emotional awareness is the ability to identify and understand our emotions. It's a critical component of self-control because it allows us to regulate our feelings effectively. When we know our emotions, we can control them to align with our goals and values.

For example, if you're frustrated or angry, you may be tempted to react impulsively, such as yelling or lashing out. However, if you're emotionally aware, you can recognize those emotions and choose to regulate them more constructively, such as taking a deep breath or using positive self-talk.

Emotional awareness also allows us to recognize when we are experiencing positive emotions, such as joy or gratitude. By identifying these emotions, we can savor and appreciate them, promoting well-being and happiness.

Strategies for Helping Children Identify and Label Emotions

1. <u>Label Emotions:</u> Children need to understand different emotions and how they feel to recognize them in themselves and others. Parents can start by labeling emotions for their children, such as "You look sad" or "You seem angry." Over time, children will begin to recognize these emotions on their own.

2. <u>Use Books and Games</u>: Children's books and games can be powerful tools for teaching emotional awareness. Choose readers and games focusing on emotions, such as "The Color Monster" by Anna Llenas or "Feelings in a Jar" by Free Spirit Publishing. These books and games can help children understand different emotions and how they feel.

3. <u>Practice Mindfulness:</u> Mindfulness is a powerful tool for promoting emotional awareness. Parents can practice mindfulness with their children through deep breathing or guided imagery. Children can become more aware of their emotions and learn to regulate them more effectively by focusing on the present moment. This is a tool that can become beneficial all through life, as problems become bigger and you're not there to rescue.

4. <u>Encourage Self-Reflection:</u> Encourage your child to reflect on their emotions throughout the day. Ask questions such as "How did you feel when you didn't get your way?" or "How did you feel when you made a mistake?" This can help children become more aware of their emotions and learn to regulate them more effectively.

5. Use Visual Aids: Visual aids, such as emotion charts or feeling faces, can be a helpful tool for teaching emotional awareness. These visual aids can help children recognize and understand their feelings. There are plenty of these available on the internet, however we have included a couple at the end.

The Role of Empathy in Teaching Emotional Awareness

Empathy is the ability to understand and share the feelings of others. It's a critical component of emotional awareness because it allows us to recognize and understand the emotions of others. By understanding the emotions of others, we can develop a deeper understanding of our own emotions and learn to regulate them more effectively. There is another book in this series that will deal directly with empathy, but we will touch on it here as it plays a role in self-control.

Empathy can be taught through a variety of strategies, including:

1. Role-Playing: Role-playing is a powerful tool for teaching empathy. Parents can role-play different scenarios with their children, such as a friend feeling sad or a classmate feeling frustrated. By taking on different perspectives, children can develop a deeper understanding of the emotions of others.

2. <u>Reading Books</u>: Children's books can be a powerful tool for teaching empathy. Choose books that focus on emotions and that tell stories from different perspectives. These books can help children understand the feelings of others and develop a more profound sense of empathy. Make sure that as you read the books, you discuss the characters' emotions and how they reacted to situations. Ask questions such as "I see Sam felt very angry in that situation; how do you think you might have felt if that happened to you?" Books are a great tool because they launch conversation. Always be sure to add much conversation with your child and ask questions to cause thinking, reasoning and conclusions.

3. <u>Encouraging Perspective-Taking</u>: Encourage your child to take the perspective of others in different situations. Ask questions like "How do you think your friend felt when you didn't share your toy?" This can help children develop a deeper understanding of the emotions of others.

4. <u>Modeling Empathy</u>: Children learn by example, so parents must model empathy in their behavior. When parents demonstrate empathy towards others, children are more likely to develop empathy themselves. Often, parents hide their emotions such as empathy however a child often learns by what they see in their caregivers so be sure to show appropriate empathy in front of your child.

Conclusion

Building emotional awareness is a critical component of self-control. By helping children identify and label emotions and by teaching empathy, parents can promote emotional awareness and help their children develop self-control. Strategies such as mindfulness, role-playing, and reading books can be powerful tools for teaching emotional awareness. By promoting emotional awareness, parents can set their children up for academic, social, and emotional success. In the following chapters, we'll explore practical strategies for promoting self-control through positive discipline and reinforcement.

Chapter 4: Developing Self-Regulation Skills

SELF-REGULATION IS THE ABILITY TO CONTROL EMOTIONS, THOUGHTS, and behaviors in a way that aligns with our goals and values. It's a critical life skill that can help children succeed academically, socially, and emotionally. In this chapter, we'll explore self-regulation and why it matters, strategies for helping children regulate their emotions and behavior, and how to address challenging behaviors and tantrums.

What Self-Regulation is and Why it Matters

Self-regulation is the ability to control our impulses, emotions, and behavior in a way that aligns with our goals and values. It's a critical life skill that can help children succeed academically, socially, and emotionally.

Self-Regulation is Essential for Several Reasons:

1. <u>Academic Success:</u> Self-regulation is associated with academic success. Children who can better regulate their emotions and behavior can focus on their studies, resist distractions, and complete their homework on time.

2. <u>Social Relationships:</u> Self-regulation is essential for developing positive social relationships. Children who can better regulate their emotions and behavior can communicate effectively, avoid conflicts, and build strong friendships.

3. <u>Emotional Well-Being</u>: Self-regulation is vital for emotional well-being. Children who can better regulate their emotions and behavior experience less stress and anxiety and better cope with challenges and setbacks.

Strategies for Helping Children Regulate Their Emotions and Behavior

1. <u>Develop a Routine:</u> Children thrive on routine and predictability. Developing a consistent routine can help children feel more secure and less anxious. Make sure your child knows what to expect throughout the day, and stick to a consistent schedule for meals, playtime, and bedtime. Rather than simply saying, "go to bed," try instead forming a particular "winding down" routine so your child can learn early to self-regulate and develop self-control. For example, this might include a non-sugared snack and drink of milk followed by a trip to the washroom, a warm face wash and a bedtime story. By allowing the child to understand the routine, you are giving them structure in which to learn self-control.

2. **Practice Mindfulness:** Mindfulness is a powerful tool for promoting self-regulation. Encourage your child to practice mindfulness through deep breathing, guided imagery, or yoga. Children can become more aware of their emotions and learn to regulate them more effectively by focusing on the present moment.

3. **Teach Coping Skills:** Coping skills, such as positive self-talk or progressive muscle relaxation, can be powerful tools for managing emotions and promoting self-regulation. Teach your child coping skills that work for them, and encourage them to use these skills when they're feeling overwhelmed or stressed. Allow your child to see you using these coping skills, whereby giving them both a verbal understanding and a visual concept of what these coping skills look like. Again, the child will model what they see.

4. **Encourage Physical Activity:** Physical activity can be a powerful tool for promoting self-regulation. Encourage your child to engage in physical activity, such as playing outside or participating in sports. Physical activity can help children burn off excess energy and regulate their emotions more effectively.

5. **Use Positive Discipline:** A positive discipline is a powerful tool for promoting self-regulation. Use redirection, natural consequences, and positive reinforcement to encourage positive behavior and reinforce self-regulation. These must be age-appropriate; redirection is a powerful tool for toddlers, while natural consequences have enormous benefits to an

older child and teen. Choose when to use which tool depending on the age of child.

How to Address Challenging Behaviors and Tantrums

Challenging behaviors and tantrums are a normal part of child development. However, they can be difficult for parents to manage. Here are some strategies for addressing problematic behaviors and tantrums all from a mindset of teaching the child self-control strategies:

1. <u>Stay Calm:</u> It's essential to stay calm when addressing challenging behaviors and tantrums. If you become upset or frustrated, your child is also more likely to become upset. Take a deep breath and try to remain calm. Furthermore, if you allow yourself an emotional outburst or response, the child will learn negative reinforcement and may later try to set off an emotional response entering into a power struggle.

2. <u>Use Positive Discipline:</u> Use positive discipline strategies to address challenging behaviors and tantrums. Techniques such as redirection, natural consequences, and positive reinforcement can effectively promote positive behavior and reinforce self-regulation. Positive discipline may include setting up a situation whereby you sit calmly at the table and eat a desirable snack, ignoring the tantrum behavior. The child will either be redirected and go to the table to share in the snack. The tantrum will have had zero results and the child will have learned that behavior does not

necessarily have desired results. Or, the child will continue in the tantrum and miss the snack; this will be a natural consequence so it is important not to get the snack back out later. Natural consequences can be difficult for a parent to allow, when it is in their power to intervene. However, natural consequences are one of a parent's most valuable tools in teaching self-control.

3. <u>Offer Choices</u>: Offering choices can effectively promote self-regulation and avoid power struggles. For example, instead of saying, "Put your shoes on," offer an option such as "Which shoes do you want to wear today?" When you offer the child a choice, they feel empowered over their own selves, initiating the beginning of autonomy. Try and offer choices to your child from very early and as often as possible, creating a safe structure for choice and self-control.

4. <u>Validate Emotions:</u> Validating your child's emotions can be a powerful tool for promoting self-regulation. Let your child know it's okay to feel upset or frustrated and offer support and understanding. Say something such as, "I can see you are feeling very angry right now and that's ok. Your feelings are important. Hitting your sister isn't a good choice in handling that anger though, so let's think of some other things you might choose next time so that your anger gets to be heard while keeping you and everyone else safe.

5. <u>Use Time-In</u>: Time-in is a positive discipline strategy involving spending time with your child when upset or misbehaving. Instead of

isolating your child as a punishment, spend time with them in a calm and supportive way. By calmly initiating an activity the child enjoys, invite them to join you.

Conclusion

Developing self-regulation skills is a critical task for parents. By using effective strategies for promoting self-regulation, such as creating a routine, practicing mindfulness, teaching coping skills, encouraging physical activity, and using positive discipline, parents can help their children develop this critical life skill. By promoting self-regulation, parents can set their children up for academic, social, and emotional success. In the following chapters, we'll explore practical strategies for boosting self-esteem and building positive relationships.

Chapter 5: Positive Discipline and Reinforcement

POSITIVE DISCIPLINE AND REINFORCEMENT ARE CRITICAL COMPONENTS OF teaching self-control. They provide children with clear expectations for behavior and encourage positive behavior through praise and rewards. In this chapter, we'll explore the importance of positive discipline and reinforcement in teaching self-control, strategies for encouraging positive behavior and reinforcing self-control, and how to address misbehavior and promote positive behavior.

The Importance of Positive Discipline and Reinforcement in Teaching Self-Control

Positive discipline and reinforcement are essential for several reasons:

1. <u>Encourages Positive Behavior:</u> Positive discipline and reinforcement encourage positive behavior by providing children with clear expectations for behavior and reinforcing positive behavior through praise and rewards. This can help children feel good about their progress and motivate them to continue practicing self-control.

2. <u>Builds Self-Esteem:</u> Positive discipline and reinforcement can help build self-esteem by giving children positive feedback and recognition for their efforts. This can help children feel good about themselves and their

abilities and install a drive for them to do their best. It's important to reward effort, not results. Since each child in a family is vastly different, one may easily be able to achieve top grades, pick up skills such as reading easily and reach what society deems as "success" without much effort, while another child in that same family might have to work three times as hard for half the results. Because children learn differently, some may have cognitive difficulties or even the differences between girls and boys and learning styles, it is important to reward effort rather than success.

3. <u>Promotes Positive Relationships:</u> Positive discipline and reinforcement can promote positive relationships between parents and children by creating a supportive and nurturing environment. When positive discipline and reinforcement are used, children are more likely to feel connected to their parents and more willing to follow the rules and expectations. When the child struggles with a particular choice, feeling or desire they will be more inclined to come and speak with a parent with whom they have built a positive, trusting relationship.

Strategies for Encouraging Positive Behavior and Reinforcing Self-Control

1. <u>Use Praise:</u> Praise is a powerful tool for encouraging positive behavior and reinforcing self-control. Praise your child when they demonstrate self-control and offer specific feedback on what they did well.

For example, "I'm so proud of you for waiting patiently while we finished our conversation." It is important not to use bribery as a regular tool, otherwise the child will learn to perform for a reward, rather than behave because they have learned self-control and right behavior. However, there is the rare time when bribery can be very impactful while avoiding a power-struggle. For example, when a child is young and required to do something they are fearful of, such as a piano recital after their first few months of lessons, they may be fearful and not want to participate. Offering a small bribe, such as sticking a coupon for lunch at their favorite restaurant on the fridge if they follow through on the recital, will not only teach them that sometimes hard things have worthwhile rewards, they will also learn to overcome unfounded fears, such as playing their piano piece in front of a few people.

2. <u>Use Rewards:</u> Rewards can be a powerful tool for reinforcing self-control. Offer rewards for positive behavior, such as earning a sticker for each day they demonstrate self-control or earning a special treat for reaching a specific goal.

3. <u>Create a Positive Environment:</u> Creating a positive environment can be a powerful tool for encouraging positive behavior and reinforcing self-control. Make sure your home is a safe and nurturing environment, and offer plenty of positive feedback and support for your child's efforts. Children thrive when they feel safe, and are nurtured on a consistent basis.

4. **Set Clear Expectations:** Set clear expectations for behavior and reinforce these expectations consistently. Ensure your child knows what is expected of them and the consequences for not meeting these expectations. Ask if they have an understanding of the boundaries around a particular area as it is discussed and welcome any questions surrounding those boundaries.

5. **Use Positive Language:** Use positive language when interacting with your child. Instead of saying, "Don't hit," say, "Be gentle." This can help reinforce positive behavior and promote self-control. Children generally like to learn and please their parents; by using positive language it will encourage the child to use self-control in their choices of behavior.

How to Address Misbehavior and Promote Positive Behavior

1. **Identify Triggers:** Identify what triggers your child's misbehavior and try to avoid these triggers when possible. For example, if your child misbehaves when hungry, ensure they have regular meals and snacks. If your child becomes combative when tired, ensure they have the needed amount of sleep and restful activities.

2. **Use Redirection:** Use redirection to encourage positive behavior and distract your child from damaging behavior. For example, if your child throws toys, redirect their attention to a different activity, and once the child is calm and some time has passed (not too much time however) have

them "help you" gather the thrown toys and have a calm conversation about some of the reasons that is not a good choice and say things such as "let's think of three other options to choose from when you feel angry and want to throw your toys." By doing this, you will give yourself more options from which to choose next time a redirection is needed and the child more options to choose from the next time they are angry.

3. **Use Natural Consequences:** Use natural consequences to reinforce positive behavior and discourage negative behavior. For example, if your child refuses to wear a coat, they may feel cold outside and learn to wear a coat in the future. The next time, a simple, "Remember the last time when you chose to wear no coat and how cold you felt?"

4. **Use Time-Outs:** Time-outs can be an effective tool for addressing misbehavior. When using time-outs, make sure they are brief and age-appropriate and explain why the time-out is happening. Keep the time-out area within eye sight so the child does not grow to learn that misbehavior results in abandonment, but rather being removed from the situation/activity.

5. **Use Positive Discipline:** Use positive discipline strategies, such as positive reinforcement and praise, to promote positive behavior and reinforce self-control, as discussed earlier.

Conclusion

Positive discipline and reinforcement are critical components of teaching self-control. Parents can help children develop these vital life skills by encouraging positive behavior and reinforcing self-control. Strategies such as using praise and rewards, creating a positive environment, and setting clear expectations can effectively promote positive behavior and strengthen self-control. Parents can use techniques such as identifying triggers, redirection, and natural consequences to promote positive behavior when addressing misbehavior. By using positive discipline and reinforcement, parents can set their children up for academic, social, and emotional success. The following chapter will explore practical strategies for promoting self-esteem and building positive relationships.

Chapter 6: Supporting Self-Control in Daily Life

Supporting self-control development in everyday situations is critical for children to learn to regulate their emotions, thoughts, and behaviors effectively, long term. In this chapter, we'll explore how to support your child's self-control development in everyday situations, strategies for promoting self-control during mealtimes, playtime, and bedtime, and the role of routines and environment in supporting self-control.

How to Support Your Child's Self-Control Development in Everyday Situations

1. <u>Model Self-Control</u>: Children learn by example, so parents must model self-control in their behavior. When parents demonstrate self-control, children are more likely to develop self-control themselves. This can range from small inconveniences such as running out of milk to large catastrophes like a hailstorm that damages your vehicle. While we all wish to lash out and respond in a big way, we must remember that we do not wish our children to react in the same way. Therefore, it is important to remember that we are model behavior we want our child to learn that will benefit them both now and later in life.

2. <u>Give Choices:</u> Giving children choices can be an effective way to promote self-control. For example, instead of telling your child what to wear, offer them a choice between two outfits. This can help your child feel more in control and develop decision-making skills. As well, it will enable your child to learn good decision making skills which will benefit them exponentially down the road of life.

3. <u>Encourage Problem-Solving</u>: Encourage your child to problem-solve in everyday situations. For example, if your child is having trouble with a toy, encourage them to find a solution independently before offering assistance. If you have children who are entangled in a battle, rather than stepping in and sending them both away, sit down in the middle of the problem. Ask them each their perspective, help them to hear what the other is saying, and then assist them in problem-solving the situation.

4. <u>Use Positive Reinforcement:</u> Use positive reinforcement, such as praise and rewards, to encourage positive behavior and reinforce self-control. For example, praise your child when they demonstrate self-control during a challenging situation.

5. <u>Talk About Emotions</u>: Talk to your child about emotions and how to regulate them effectively. Encourage your child to identify feelings and practice coping skills like deep breathing or positive self-talk, rather than telling them how to feel.

Strategies for Promoting Self-Control During Mealtimes, Playtime, and Bedtime

1. <u>Mealtimes</u>: Mealtimes can be a challenging time for children to practice self-control. Encourage your child to practice self-control by offering healthy food choices and encouraging them to wait until everyone is seated before beginning to eat. Include them in mealtime conversations give opportunities to use self-control, as you model self-control.

2. <u>Playtime</u>: Playtime can be an excellent opportunity for children to practice self-control. Encourage your child to take turns and share toys with others. Offer positive reinforcement when your child demonstrates self-control during playtime.

3. <u>Bedtime</u>: Bedtime can be challenging for children to practice self-control. Encourage your child to wind down before bedtime by engaging in calming activities, such as reading a book or taking a bath. Set clear expectations for bedtime routines and enforce them consistently, as we've discussed in a previous chapter.

The Role of Routines and Environment in Supporting Self-Control

1. <u>Routines</u>: Routines can be a powerful tool for promoting self-control. Make sure your child knows what to expect throughout the day and stick

to a consistent schedule for meals, playtime, and bedtime. This can help children feel more secure and less anxious.

2. <u>Environment</u>: The environment can play a significant role in supporting self-control. Create a safe and nurturing environment that promotes positive behavior and encourages self-regulation. Avoid overstimulation and limit distractions to help your child focus and regulate their emotions effectively.

3. <u>Limit Screen Time</u>: Limiting screen time can be an effective way to promote self-control. Excessive screen time can lead to overstimulation and make it more difficult for children to regulate their emotions and behavior effectively.

4. <u>Encourage Physical Activity:</u> Physical activity can be a powerful tool for promoting self-control. Physical activity can help children burn off excess energy and regulate their emotions more effectively.

Conclusion

Supporting self-control development in everyday situations is critical for children to learn to regulate their emotions, thoughts, and behaviors effectively. Strategies such as modeling self-control, giving choices, encouraging problem-solving, using positive reinforcement, and talking about feelings can effectively promote self-control. Parents can encourage self-control during mealtimes, playtime, and bedtime by offering healthy food choices, facilitating sharing and taking turns during playtime, and setting clear expectations for bedtime routines. The role of routines and environment is also critical in supporting self-control. Parents can help their children develop self-control and succeed in academic, social, and emotional domains by creating a safe and nurturing environment, limiting distractions, and encouraging physical activity. In the following chapter, we'll explore strategies for promoting resilience and coping skills in children.

Chapter 7: Nurturing Self-Esteem and Resilience

SELF-ESTEEM AND RESILIENCE ARE CRITICAL COMPONENTS OF A CHILD'S emotional health and development. They are closely related to self-control, as children with high self-esteem and resilience can better regulate their emotions, thoughts, and behaviors effectively. This chapter will explore how self-esteem and resilience relate to self-control, strategies for promoting self-esteem and resilience in young children, and how to foster a growth mindset.

How Self-Esteem and Resilience Relate to Self-Control

Self-esteem and resilience are closely related to self-control. Children with high self-esteem and resilience can better regulate their emotions, thoughts, and behaviors effectively. They are more likely to persist in facing challenges and setbacks and less likely to give up or engage in negative behavior.

Self-esteem is the way we feel about ourselves and our abilities. Children with high self-esteem are more likely to have a positive self-image, feel confident in their abilities, and be willing to take calculated risks.

Resilience is the ability to bounce back from challenges and setbacks. Resilient children are better able to cope with stress and adversity. They are more likely to persevere in the face of obstacles.

Both self-esteem and resilience are essential for promoting self-control. Children with high self-esteem and resilience can better regulate their emotions, thoughts, and behaviors effectively and are more likely to succeed in academic, social, and emotional domains.

Strategies for Promoting Self-Esteem and Resilience in Young Children

1. <u>Encourage Positive Self-Talk</u>: Encourage your child to use positive self-talk to boost their self-esteem and resilience. Teach your child to replace negative thoughts with positive ones, such as "I can do this" or "I am capable."

2. <u>Praise Effort</u>: Praise effort rather than just the result. This can help your child feel good about their progress and motivate them to continue trying, even in the face of challenges. Effort is what brings success and should be both encouraged and praised.

3. <u>Encourage Perseverance:</u> Encourage your child to persevere in the face of challenges and setbacks. Help your child develop problem-solving skills and offer support and encouragement when they face obstacles. Book five in this series that deals specifically with this subject.

4. <u>Provide Opportunities for Success:</u> Provide your child with opportunities for success. Offer age-appropriate challenges and activities

your child can succeed in, and offer positive feedback and recognition for their efforts. The more a child experiences some levels of success, the more they will find they make choices that will lead to more success.

5. <u>Foster Connections:</u> Foster positive connections with family, friends, and community. Positive relationships can help children feel supported and connected, boosting their self-esteem and resilience. Ensure plenty of quality time is spent with positive people, both adults in the child's life and children with whom they enjoy spending time.

How to Foster a Growth Mindset in Children

A growth mindset believes that hard work and dedication can develop abilities and intelligence. Children with a growth mindset are more likely to persevere in the face of challenges and setbacks, take risks, and try new things.

Here are some strategies for fostering a growth mindset in children:

1. <u>Encourage a Love of Learning:</u> Encourage your child to enjoy learning and see challenges as growth opportunities. This can be by doing activities together such as going to the park and choosing a favorite leaf to bring home and study or craft with or looking at bugs outside, then coming inside and researching that bug. The child will quickly love these activities and foster a love of learning.

2. **Praise Effort:** Praise your child's effort rather than the result. This can help your child see that hard work and dedication are essential for success. Define success for your child, not by money or fame, but by achieved results and best effort.

3. **Encourage Risk-Taking:** Encourage your child to take risks and try new things. Help your child develop problem-solving skills and offer support and encouragement when they face obstacles. Let them see you try new things and have them share in the experience of joy and satisfaction upon completing these experiences, nurturing the desire to try new things for themselves.

4. **Teach Persistence:** Teach your child to persist in facing challenges and setbacks. Help them develop problem-solving skills and offer support and encouragement when they face obstacles. Book 5 in this series deals more in-depth on this topic.

5. **Model a Growth Mindset:** Model a growth mindset in your behavior. Show your child that you value hard work and dedication and are willing to take risks and try new things.

Conclusion

Self-esteem and resilience are critical components of a child's emotional health and development. They are closely related to self-control, as children with high self-esteem and resilience can better regulate their emotions, thoughts, and behaviors effectively. Strategies such as encouraging positive self-talk, praising effort, encouraging perseverance, providing opportunities for success, and fostering connections can effectively promote self-esteem and resilience in young children. Cultivating a growth mindset in children can also encourage self-control, as children with a growth mindset are likelier to persevere in facing challenges and setbacks. Parents can set their children up for success in academic, social, and emotional domains by promoting self-esteem, resilience, and a growth mindset. The following chapter will explore strategies for fostering positive relationships between parents and children.

Wrapping it Up:

This book explored the importance of teaching self-control to young children. We discussed how self-control is critical for success in academic, social, and emotional domains and how parents can support their children's self-control development through positive discipline and reinforcement, supporting self-control in daily life, and nurturing self-esteem and resilience. Some key points from the book include:

- Self-control is critical for academic, social, and emotional success.

- Positive discipline and reinforcement can encourage positive behavior and reinforce self-control.
- Supporting self-control in daily life can be achieved through routines, environment, and promoting positive behavior during mealtimes, playtime, and bedtime.
- Self-esteem and resilience are closely related to self-control, and parents can promote these qualities in their children through positive self-talk, praise of effort, perseverance, providing opportunities for success, and fostering connections.
- Fostering a growth mindset can also promote self-control, as children with a growth mindset are more likely to persevere in the face of challenges and setbacks.

Teaching self-control to young children is a challenging but critical task for parents. By using the strategies and techniques discussed in this book, parents can help their children develop self-control, setting them up for academic, social, and emotional success.

Final Thoughts:

Teaching self-control to young children is an ongoing process that requires patience, consistency, and dedication. Parents must remember that self-control development is a journey, and setbacks and challenges are natural.Parents can support their children's self-control development by providing a safe and nurturing environment, setting clear expectations for behavior, and using positive discipline and reinforcement. Remembering self-control is closely related to self-esteem, and resilience is also important. Parents can promote these qualities in their children through positive self-talk, praise of effort, perseverance, providing opportunities for success, and fostering connections.

Additional Resources for Parents

Many resources are available for parents who want to learn more about teaching self-control to young children.

- "No-Drama Discipline" by Daniel J. Siegel and Tina Payne Bryson
- "Positive Discipline" by Jane Nelsen
- "How to Talk So Kids Will Listen & Listen So Kids Will Talk" by Adele Faber and Elaine Mazlish
- "The Whole-Brain Child" by Daniel J. Siegel and Tina Payne Bryson
- "The Power of Positive Parenting" by Glenn Latham

In addition, parents can access online resources, such as parenting blogs, podcasts, and forums, to connect with other parents and gain additional insights and support.

Kid's books to drive the point home:

"The Giving Tree" by Shel Silverstein - This story is about a tree that gives everything it has to a boy throughout his life, showing the importance of generosity and selflessness.

"It's OK to Cry" by Kimm Reid - A conversation between a young girl and her dolly, Annabelle. The story shares how the young girl experiences numerous feelings such as fear, sadness, anger, joy, and jealousy through different events and how Annabelle teaches her that while it's ok to feel the feelings, she can't let them own her or control her. "You are the boss of your feelings," Annabelle reminds her. "Your feelings are not the boss of you."

Worksheets:

1. Emotion Identification Worksheet:

   There are many worksheets available online to help children learn to identify emotions, which is an important first step-in developing self-control. We have included two here, but if you'd like to find more, they are simple to find or create yourself.

Draw a line from the face to the word it fits with.

1. Emotion: _____
2. Emotion: _____
3. Emotion: _____
4. Emotion: _____
5. Emotion: _____
6. Emotion: _____
7. Emotion: _____
8. Emotion: _____

Reflection: After completing the worksheet, take a moment to reflect on your own emotions. Have you experienced any of the emotions you identified on the worksheet? If so, when and in what context? How did you respond to those emotions? Are there any emotions that you find challenging to identify or express?

This worksheet can be used as a tool for developing emotional intelligence and awareness. By identifying and reflecting on different emotions, your children can learn to better understand their own emotions and the emotions of others, which can improve communication, relationships, and overall well-being.

2. Self-Talk Worksheet ideas: This worksheet can help children develop positive self-talk, which is an important tool for promoting self-control. The worksheet can include different scenarios and ask children to write down positive statements they can tell themselves in each scenario.

   A. Positive Self-Talk: Encourage your child to practice positive self-talk with this worksheet. Help them identify negative thoughts and reframe them into positive ones. Use the following prompts:
   - What negative thoughts do you have about yourself?
   - How can you turn those negative thoughts into positive ones?
   - Write down three positive affirmations to say to yourself when you are feeling down.

   B. Coping Skills Self-Talk:
   Teach your child coping skills with this worksheet. Help them identify their emotions and use positive self-talk to manage them. Use the following prompts:
   - What emotions do you feel when you are upset?
   - How can you calm yourself down when you are feeling upset?
   - Write down three positive affirmations to say to yourself when you are feeling upset.

C. Goal-Setting Self-Talk:

Encourage your child to set goals and use positive self-talk to achieve them with this worksheet. Use the following prompts:

- What goals do you want to achieve?
- What positive self-talk can you use to motivate yourself to achieve those goals?
- Write down three positive affirmations to say to yourself when working towards your goals.

These self-talk worksheet ideas can help your child develop positive self-talk habits, cope with difficult emotions, and achieve their goals.

Made in the USA
Monee, IL
28 April 2026